Dogs Get It

Advice I Learned From My Best Friend

Written by Mike Messeroff
Illustrated by Hannah Rose Chavez

Dogs Get It
Advice I Learned From My Best Friend

Published by Happy As Dog LLC
Copyright © 2019 Happy As Dog LLC. All rights reserved.

Written by Mike Messeroff

Illustrated by Hannah R. Chavez
Cover design and illustration by Hannah R. Chavez
Book design by Hannah R. Chavez

Names: Messeroff, Mike, author. | Chavez, Hannah R., illustrator.
Title: Dogs get it : advice I learned from my best friend / written by Mike Messeroff ; illustrated by Hannah R. Chavez.
Description: Breckenridge, CO: Happy As a Dog, LLC, 2019.
Identifiers: LCCN 2019919836 | ISBN 978-1-7343253-1-7 (Hardcover) | 978-1-7343253-0-0 (pbk.)
Subjects: LCSH Dogs--Pictorial works. | Dogs--Anecdotes. | Human-animal relationships--Anecdotes. | Self-actualization (Psychology) | Success--Psychological aspects. | BISAC SELF-HELP / Motivational & Inspirational | BODY, MIND & SPIRIT / Inspiration & Personal Growth | PETS / Dogs / General
Classification: LCC SF426.2 .M47 2019 | DDC 636.7088--dc23

BULK ORDERS: We are happy to offer special terms for schools, companies, professional groups, clubs, and other organizations when ordering quantities of this title. For information, please email hi@happyasdog.com.

This book is printed in the United States of America.
Created with love in Breckenridge, CO and New York, NY.

Happy Birthday
Merry Christmas
2020

To: Janet

From: Mary Js

Acknowledgments

There are so many people who helped make this a reality. Hannah, this book was so much fun creating with you and simply would not be what it is without you and your talents. Dave, for your unwavering support, ideas, evolving together, and for being the *other* best friend. Amy, it's been amazing going through a similar spiritual journey as my sister and being able to share and grow together. Lauren H., Kelsey, Dani, Laurel, Izzi, Lauren F., and all of my fellow Summit County Mindful Manifestors...your support and guidance have been life-changing. Devin, for introducing me to *The Four Agreements* and setting me on my path of growth and awakening. Mom, Cara, and all family and friends, as well as Schweitz, Friedy, Guapo, and Seth for their professional insight. To new friends and perfect strangers who have generously offered their time and experiences to help with the creation of this book. Rocky and all the real-life dogs who inspired the illustrated dogs on these pages. The mentors who have all changed my life, including Alan Watts, Esther Hicks, Andy Puddicombe, Eckhart Tolle, Dr. Wayne Dyer, Dr. Joe Dispenza, Rev. Ike. and all of you out there creating more of this content to be shared and enjoyed. For everyone who reads this book, practices this wisdom in your life, and shares the message with others.

Thank you all.

Finally, to Alisa...I never believed in angels until the day I realized I am married to one. Your passion for life, uplifting attitude, guidance, bravery, individuality, and support has helped me become the person I am today and I can never thank you enough.

Dedication

To Rocky...my son and best friend.
You really do get it, and I'm grateful that I finally caught on.

Enjoy the wind in your face.

Dogs and humans alike

want to be free and at ease.

So roll down

your window

and take in that breeze…

Bask in the sunlight.

A moment spent
    basking in the sun,
is a moment savored
    long after it's done.

Stretch every day.

Listen to your body.

Move, stretch, wriggle, be free!

Dogs do this instinctively...

Shouldn't we?

Wake up excited.

Happy dogs know that each new day,
can mean an adventure is on the way.
So if you wish to wake up eager,
to live life and not just get through it,
figure out what makes you happy
and invest time to make sure that you do it!

Kiss a lot.

When it comes to affection,
some give hugs...others give licks.
However you do it, show you care often...
and make it a habit that sticks.

YOU

are

the

only one

who

knows

what

you're

thinking.

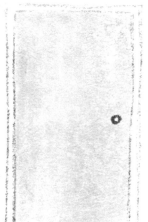

Dogs do this naturally,

and don't take any credit.

So make it clear what you want,

and you'll usually get it.

Spread joy.

If all you give today

is a nod or a smile,

you'll make someone's day,

and you'll do it with style.

Be quick to make friends.

If it feels right, go ahead and **take a chance**.

Remember, we all need partners because *life is a dance*.

Be yourself.

The only approval you need is your own.

So be who you are *meant to be*...

You are not a clone!

You **can** teach an old dog new tricks.

If you always do what you've always done, your mind isn't growing or having much fun. So learn something new, it's never too late. Be a creator...take control of your fate.

Greet like you mean it.

What a

wonderful gift

to bestow,

when you are

happy to

see someone...

Let

them

know!

WELCOME

Find

something

you

are

passionate

about.

If your *work* feels like play,

It isn't work at all...wouldn't you say?

Make time.

If you had but ten or twenty years on this earth,

how much more would each day be worth?

Life is an hourglass...we don't know how much sand remains above.

So do the things that make you happy and spend time with the ones you love.

Be the best friend
you want to have.

You attract in

what you radiate out.

So be the kind of friend

you would rave about.

Be loyal, up for adventure,

and a good listener, too.

Otherwise, what kind of friends

are you attracting to you?

Trust your gut.

Guidance is always there...

deep down you already know.

Pay attention

to the way you feel,

and you'll know

which direction to go.

Make it a priority to have fun.

Even when you think

you're too busy,

stop and make

time to play.

Get up,

move around,

or spend time with

a friend...it may be

the best thing you do all day!

What
you
are doing
is what **matters**.

Whether you're keeping busy or taking time to be lazy,

comparing yourself to others will only make you crazy.

When you realize there's no race to win, nor anyone to beat,

you can define what makes you happy...

there's no reason to compete.

There is power beyond words.

How can dogs "say" so much without speaking a word?

And yet, you know how they feel even when

nothing is heard.

So use your body language

and connect with your eyes...

It's amazing what you can do

simply with your energy and vibes.

Bring

out

the

puppy

in

you.

When did it all get so complicated?

Perhaps growing up is a little overrated?

Figure out what makes you feel like a kid,

and go do it often…you'll be glad that you did.

Focus on the good.

Every time you catch yourself
about to complain,
remember that it will only be
an energy drain.

Then make a **choice** to focus
on the **good** instead,
because your **reality** is created from
the **thoughts** in your head.

Get

comfortable

with

being

uncomfortable.

The road less traveled exists just for you...

so go ahead and be open; try something new!

It isn't personal.

The next time something happens and you feel offended,
take solace in knowing it's likely not what was intended.
Be quick to forgive, and choose to be kind...
you'll be amazed at the incredible power you find.

The present moment
is all we *ever* have.

Are you being **mindful**, or is your mind simply **full**?

Take note when you get **lost** in thought,

and practice **letting go** of that **pull**.

Be grateful.

Say thank you from the moment you start your day,

and then for your blanket and the bed where you lay.

Be thankful for it all, it's the best attitude.

You'll attract more good into your life,

simply with gratitude.

Appreciate
the
differences
in
others.

Most dogs love other dogs,

regardless of looks or breed.

Can you say the same of other humans,

regardless of race, nationality, or creed?

You have to admit, it would be pretty lame,

if every dog, and every human,

were exactly the same.

Quiet your mind.

Dogs waste no energy on time ahead or already past,
blissfully content from the first hour of the day to the last.
So forget all that you think and all that you know,
if you're not quieting your mind you're missing most of the show.
Instead of being your thoughts, you step back and observe,
and instead of obeying them, it's you who they serve.

More Resources

We had so much fun making this book and really hope that you have just as much fun reading it and sharing it with friends and loved ones.

If you would like to learn more about any of the subject matter covered in the book, such as meditation, mindfulness, practicing gratitude, manifesting, and more, please check out MikeMesseroff.com and follow @MikeMesseroff on Instagram for daily inspiration.

Author
Mike Messeroff

After spending ten years behind a corporate desk in New York City, and several more years as a world-traveling bartender, Mike Messeroff now lives in Breckenridge, Colorado and enjoys the outdoors, travel, and spending time with his wife, friends, his best friend/Yorkshire Terrier "Rocky" (the inspiration behind this book and our cover model), and his new puppy "Lela". As Mike began discovering the world of mindfulness and spirituality, he realized that Rocky was naturally exhibiting some of the greatest life skills and habits and that we could all learn a lot from our four-legged friends. Mike is also a Personal Freedom Coach, helping others to discover and actualize their greatest desires, and is excited to be sharing his experiences, tips, videos, and new projects on MikeMesseroff.com. Be sure to check it out and join the community!

Illustrator
Hannah Rose Chavez

Originally from New York City, Hannah developed a love of art from a young age, along with an understanding of its impact in the world. She spent the last several years in the mountains of Colorado, gaining insights and finding her voice as an artist. Currently back in New York, Hannah is focusing on her two main passions: art and animals. Having grown up with cats and dogs, she has always felt a deep connection with animals, and is presently accompanied through life by her beloved cat, Mowgli. Working as a freelance artist, and using her personal artwork to spread awareness about animal welfare and conservation issues, Hannah has found a way to combine her passions into a purposeful career. A portion of her art profits is also donated to animal rescue organizations. To see more of her work, visit her website at: hannahchavezart.com.